CW01305332

IT'S NOT YOUR FAULT
True Stories of Abused Women
©2015 William H. Joiner, Jr.

All rights reserved. No part of this publication may be reproduced or used in any form or by any means, graphic, electronic or mechanical, including photocopying, recording, taping, or information and retrieval systems without written permission of the publisher.

Edited by Missy Brewer
Book design by Michael Campbell, MCWriting.com
Cover design by Bryan Gehrke, MyCoverDesigner.com
ISBN: 978-1519781536

90% of the net profits from this book will be donated to organizations which help abused women.

For more information visit www.williamjoinerauthor.com

"The first time he hit me we were at a dance. I was talking to another guy at the bar. Benny came up behind me, turned me around, and slammed a beer bottle into my face." — MARY

"When I found out I was pregnant, I thought we would be a big happy family. That all ended when he got drunk and kicked me in the stomach. I miscarried." — MARTHA

"He went on to tell me 'if you ever tell anyone our secret, I will tell them that you are the one who asked for this.' Naturally, only being nine years old, I had no idea what he really meant, but I will never forget what happened next." — PAULA

"Upon moving to our new home there were new rules. I was allowed no car and no phone, as before. But now I was also not allowed shoes so I could not run away. If I did everything right and didn't make him angry, he would allow me to buy food." — ASHLEY

When William Joiner was asked to write the true story of an abused woman, he put out a call for the personal experiences of other women who had suffered abuse. Stunned by the vast, gut-wrenching responses, he vowed to write this broader account of their stories, in order to give hope, courage and resources to women in need.

IT'S NOT YOUR FAULT

TRUE STORIES OF ABUSED WOMEN

WILLIAM H. JOINER, JR.

CONTENTS

Foreword . . . . *ix*

The Story of Mary *11*

The Story of Lisa. *21*

The Story of Dixie *25*

The Story of Martha *31*

The Story of Sue Ellen *35*

The Story of Lynn *39*

The Story of Angela *43*

The Story of Vivian *49*

The Story of Helen *53*

The Story of Paula *57*

The Story of Ashley. *63*

The Author Weighs In. *79*

How do I get help? *81*

Acknowledgements *83*

Other books by William Joiner. . . *85*

FOREWORD

I was asked to write the true story of an abused woman. Even though I had nine books in print, I was initially resistant because my experience as an author had primarily been in fiction. When I decided to go forward with the book, I put out a call for the personal experiences of women who had suffered abuse. I was stunned at the response. A large percentage of the women I spoke with had either experienced abuse or had a family member or friend who had.

Of course, I knew that many women dealt with various forms of abuse: physical, sexual, mental and verbal. But, the firsthand reports were gut-wrenching. With this book, I hope to shine a brighter light on this blight on humanity. It will also provide real resources for abused women to be able to get the help they need.

I have reported the stories in this book almost verbatim as they were sent to me, although I had to edit some for clarity. Punctuation or spelling is not as important as the reader hearing the voices of these women. I have changed the names and locations to protect their privacy.

90% of the net profits from this book will be donated to organizations which help abused women.

Mary

THE STORY OF
MARY

· · · · · · · · · · · · · · · · · · ·

I married my high school sweetheart. We started dating the July between our sophomore and junior years. He was a cowboy who wore a big, black hat, he liked to two-step, and he thought I was the prettiest thing he'd ever seen. Looking back, I always thought I was a little bit better than him, but I could mold him and change him into exactly what I though he needed to be. We partied like typical high school students in the 80's – beer, bon fires, and Friday night dances. The natural progression of things happened as expected: we graduated, he asked my Dad's permission to marry me the next December, and we got married that next June.

Yep, we were 19 and were going to conquer the world. And then I did the stupidest thing I've ever done in my life: I brought a joint home to smoke with him. I've regretted that decision every single day of my life. It was a whole new world to him. He started the hunt for the next high. He ended up getting a DWI, lost his driver's license, and so we moved to Texas. It was just us. Both of our families lived in New Orleans, Louisiana, and so we were all alone.

For a few weeks, we stayed with a couple who had known one of our older siblings. The husband turned Benny on to cocaine. I did it some too, but it changed him. We had had fights before, but things started getting serious. He started pushing me.

The first time he hit me we were at a dance. I was talking to another guy at the bar. Benny came up behind me, turned me around, and slammed a beer bottle into my face. It busted my lips wide open and blackened my eyes. The cops were called. They wanted to arrest him, but by this point he was very sorry, so I wouldn't press charges. My friend who was with us ended up calling my parents and telling them what happened. I defended Benny and told my parents that it was all a misunderstanding. I told my co-workers I was hit in the face while playing softball. I'm sure they didn't believe me.

By this time, he would do any drug he could find and drink any alcohol he had at the time. He would rage like you can't imagine. He would take my car to work and make me walk to humiliate me. He started treating me like I was less than—less than what? Less than everything.

We stayed in Texas until 1989, then we decided to move home. I didn't realize at that point how hard it was going to be to hide our life from our families.

But this is part of the crazy: my dad would do anything in the world to protect me. If I told the things that were going on with Benny, my dad would hate him. I had no plan of leaving him (because I could still fix him) and I wanted my family to love him. The drugs continued, the drinking continued, and I didn't tell. I was embarrassed. So I didn't tell. I was ashamed. So I didn't tell. Instead, I got pregnant. I had the most beautiful, perfect baby girl. I mean surely he would change now—he's a dad! He didn't. Instead, he learned manipulation. He learned how to hurt me without lifting a hand. Thus began the mental game: fat ass, lard ass, ugly, nobody would want you, you're not worth anything. He would disappear for days at a time. But he was always sorry.

And remember…I was going to change him…? He once left to go to the video store. He was gone for a week. He was arrested for breaking in someone's door. I was so relieved that he was in jail. I slept like a baby for two nights. When he came back, though, the real physical violence started. He would pull my hair, whack me in the head, and push me into stuff. Not every day, not even every week. But I was afraid of him.

So… I finally told one person: the lady who watched my daughter while I worked. I filed a restraining order and the judge granted it the same day. I was afraid to see him, so the police served him at our house while I wasn't there. He had to leave. Thank you, Jesus!!! This little piece of paper will keep him away!! Because if he violates it, he will be breaking the law and will be arrested again!!!! Right??? No. It doesn't really work like that. And anyways, he was *really* sorry this time. He was going to change. He never meant to hurt me. He actually went to rehab for 28 days. Best 28 days I had had in a long, long time. And then he called me and told me to bring him a joint to rehab. I said, "Seriously?" He told me he would leave me if I didn't. Manipulation via telephone while in rehab. It happened, people! But I did it and I stayed with him… *because I was changing him!!!!*

So I had another baby. A baby boy, his namesake, he would carry on the family name. But no… no change at all. So I was in a severely abusive relationship and had a toddler and a baby. And no one knew. He would leave us for days at a time. And no one knew. He once took us all to eat at Burger King, and then he took off in the car and just left us there. And never came back. Alone at a fast food joint with my kids and no car. I can't call anyone for a ride… because what would I tell them?

Everything escalated quickly when he finally got home. I told him to leave over and over again. I actually pointed a gun at him one night. But he just laughed at me. He left one night and I was so afraid of him, I called my brother. My brother didn't ask any questions. He just came to my house and sat in the living room with a baseball bat. Benny laughed at me, as usual, when he finally came home. Then he went to rehab #2.

When he came home, nothing changed. One very ordinary day, I went to pick up the kids at day care and went home. Benny was waiting for me just inside the door. He picked me up and threw me into a gun cabinet. Glass broke; shards fell all over my kids. Miraculously, no one was cut. So this time, I was done. Finished. Over it. Now came restraining order #2. He actually moved out of the house. But he told me that he would come back and burn the house down. I put solid metal doors on my house because I was afraid he would kick the doors in. He told me he would take the kids, he would kill me, he would burn the house down.

I finally divorced him. And still my family didn't know much. Thank God I removed my kids and me from that horrible situation. Ha! It wasn't over. Benny would sit outside my house and just watch. Watch and wait and plan. I started dating a guy I met at work. We married. He brought two girls to the marriage and I brought my two kids, so we were a blended family of six.

Benny would come and go, appear and disappear. One day it had snowed so my husband drove me to work. My son had stayed with his dad that day, so Benny met me at the end of the work day to leave my son with me. My son and I got into my husband's truck. I didn't put my son in his car seat because he was asleep. We're driving down an icy road and come up to a stop light. My husband eases to a stop, and WHACK! We're rear-ended. It was Benny. He purposely ran into the truck my son and I were in. He just stared at us with cold, dark eyes.

The kids would go months without seeing him. He moved to northern Louisiana where he was arrested for battery on a household member and holding someone against their will. His dad paid the fine. He did a few weeks in jail and moved back to New Orleans.

He really didn't bother us much. He would come to my son's baseball games and my daughter's softball games sometimes. He would say things to me that only I could hear: "I love you," "you're still mine," "I won't let you go." Creepy, scary things. Then he would disappear again. Then reappear.

So our lives continued, our kids grew, my marriage was great. I heard that Benny was using meth and that he was in a dark place. Then came a day that I'll never forget. It was a Sunday. My son and I saw Benny around 6 that evening. I went to pick up child support. He was already so drunk and high. He told me he still loved me. I knew the look in his eyes, so I just left.

School was starting for the kids the next day. The next day also happened to be my daughter's and one of my husband's daughter's birthdays! So we were all in bed and the phone rings. It's 11:58 at night. I answer the phone. It's Benny so I just hand the phone to my husband. My husband's end of the conversation goes something like this: "We're sleeping. You're drunk. Go home and sleep it off. No, I won't meet you at the park." My husband hangs up. Benny immediately calls back and tells me he's going to burn our house down and kill us all. If he can't have me, no one can.

My husband jumps out of bed. He tells me that Benny was coming to the house and he wanted to fight. I told my husband to be careful because I was sure Benny would have a gun, and I called 911. It doesn't ring. I hang up and call again. It doesn't ring. I run to grab the other phone and call again. This time it works. I tell the dispatcher the story and to send someone over. She keeps me on the phone.

Benny comes from the alley in his truck. My husband yells at Benny to go home. Benny gets out of his truck, but leaves the door to his truck open. He runs up to my husband and starts kicking and throwing punches with one hand. My husband pushes him back to his truck. Benny reaches into the cab of his truck and pulls out a gas can. He yells that he's going to burn the house down. He douses my husband with gasoline and has a lighter in his other hand. My husband had put a knife in his back pocket on his way out the door. My husband stabs Benny in the gut. Benny gets back in his truck and drives off. As he's driving off, he looks at me and says ,"I'll be back."

Later that morning we learned that he had gotten about a mile away, and he crashed into a fence. The ambulance gets to the wreck. They can't stop the bleeding from the wound in his stomach because his blood is so thin from the alcohol. They get him to the hospital. He goes into surgery. He dies at 4:00 a.m. on the operating table. We didn't learn about this until later that morning.

So a few days after this, I took my kids to their dad's funeral. Their dad's family wanted us to sit with them. I know they were confused and hurting, but they hadn't done a damn thing to help Benny. His mom and his sister had practically disowned him. His dad let him live with him and knew exactly how messed up he was.

The next 18 months are what I call "The months of fog." Remembering it is like looking through water. My husband was arrested, charged with first-degree murder. We prepared for a trial. The truth was all we had, so that's the story we told. My family still didn't know how bad the abuse had been because I had not told them. They just didn't understand how this could have happened. The trial date was set. Our kids were 7, 8, 9, and 11. They had to go to school. They had to be interviewed by the DA. It was worse than any nightmare I could imagine. The state dismissed the charges the Thursday before the trial was to start and ruled it justifiable homicide.

We left Louisiana and never looked back. Come to find out, Benny had been parked in our alley that night for about five hours. He was watching our house. They found cigarette butts, an empty bottle of Jack Daniels, beer bottles, and syringes. His blood alcohol content was .29. He has meth in his system and more meth in his pockets. He had told people he had had my husband and me in his crosshairs on more than one occasion. Total. Devastation. I couldn't even speak God's name.

I'm not sure how I functioned, but I did. It's been 13 years, and I still live with so much guilt. If I would've been brave enough to tell my dad, he would've protected me. My kids get to live with the fact that their stepdad killed their dad. They all know the truth. No one could make this stuff up. But how I wish I would've known that there was no changing him.

I wish I knew where to go, who to tell, what to do. I wish there were cell phones with apps for domestic violence. I wish there was the universal knowledge that a black dot in the center of a woman's hand was a sign that she was being abused. But there's so much shame, so much embarrassment, so much humiliation. The abuse doesn't have to win. God was always there with me. I didn't always realize it, but looking back I know He is my salvation in many, many ways. He saved me from being killed many times, and He saved me from suffocating from this all-encompassing guilt. My husband's story is miraculous, but it's not my story to tell.

I read the book *The Shack* about eight years ago. It changed my life. So... I have a God who is especially fond of me, a husband who loves me and works tirelessly to provide for me, four amazing adult children, and my first grandbaby due in a few months. My life is good.

This is my advice: make a plan to leave, even if it's only in your head. Tell someone, anyone. Put a black dot in the middle of your hand. There are people who love you and who will help you. They don't have to understand your story. And remember, "the leaving" is the most dangerous part. Be aware and stay in control!

Lisa

THE STORY OF
LISA

I AM ASHAMED TO ADMIT that I had two abusive relationships before I was able have a healthy relationship. Recognizing the relationships were abusive was the first step towards healing. Initially, each time I began a new relationship, I always thought it would be different. I was so desperate to be loved that I was blind to the fact that each one was going down the same path.

I was only 14 when I had my first real boyfriend, Scott, who was 18. By real, I mean the relationship was sexual. Everything was great as long as I did what he wanted, when he wanted it.

I was already depressed due to my family life. My mom and dad were alcoholics. There were times when there was no food in the house because all the money had been spent on beer. I wasn't stupid. I could see that my family was different from most of the families that my friends from school had.

I had to be loved. I saw Scott as my only option. I knew things weren't right, but what other choice did I have? Even though Scott was never satisfied with anything I did, he took over my life. It was like I was in jail and he was the sheriff. When we went out in public, I tried to shrink into the background. I didn't want anyone to notice me, especially Scott.

One of the worst things he did was to take away my friends. Scott said, "Stay away from any guys. All they want is to screw you. The girls that you call friends are lezbos. They want in your pants too. I'm the only one you can trust. I'll take care of you." I wasn't allowed to talk to anyone.

My feelings were split. Sometimes I felt such intense pain that I thought I couldn't stand it. Other times, I was numb. I felt nothing. I just didn't give a shit about anything.

I had a hard time admitting that Scott didn't give a shit about me even though he never gave me a present for my birthday or for Christmas. A counsellor at school heard about how Scott was treating me. She tried to tell me that he was just using me, but I didn't care what she said. I couldn't face life without Scott. I had no one else. I know it sounds crazy now, but I felt so worthless, I thought Scott was doing me a favor by putting up with me.

Scott began to attack me physically. The most serious was when he strangled me hard enough that it left marks around my neck. I wore a scarf to hide them. He never apologized. He told me, "Quit pissing me off and I'll stop hitting you. You deserve what you're getting." Scott became physically abusive during sex. He would slap me if he thought I wasn't doing it right.

Our relationship lasted for three years. I was completely submissive to him, but nothing helped. I could never satisfy him. All I heard was how stupid I was and how lucky I was that he put up with me. Scott finally got bored with me and left. I cried for four days. I thought my life was over.

It took me all of two weeks to find another boyfriend through an internet dating service. Neal had a different personality from Scott so I thought things would also be different. He held his momma up to me as an example. Neal wanted me to dress like her and talk like her. He ridiculed me when I didn't measure up to his momma.

What made it even crazier was his momma barely tolerated him. I could see that she didn't care if he was around or not. Neal idolized his momma and she seemed to despise him.

Neal never hit me, but it was a never-ending barrage of mental abuse. He badgered me continually about everything that he was insecure about. He would ask me every day, "Tell me again why you should be my girlfriend? You're not pretty enough or smart enough to be with me. Why should I keep you around?"

I finally realized why he wanted me to look and talk like his momma. She hated him so Neal wanted me to take her place. He could control me. He couldn't control his momma. The final straw was when I found some porn videos showing mothers with their sons. I still loved him, but was filled with disgust. Feelings have a mind of their own. I can't explain it.

I am proud of myself that I got out of that relationship. I was waitressing at a local café. I had made friends with another waitress, Debbie. One day we took off early and went to the tiny apartment Neal and I shared. Debbie and I packed my shit and I moved in with her.

Neal came by the café a couple of times saying he needed to talk with me to tell me how sorry he was. Now that I was out, I didn't want anything to do with him. The last time he came by, Debbie screamed at him that if he didn't quit bothering me, she was going to call the cops. Neal never tried to see me again. Deep down I always knew he was a coward.

If there's one thing I would tell other women, it is to trust your gut. I always knew that Scott and Neal were bad apples, but I thought I could change them. I couldn't.

Dixie

THE STORY OF
DIXIE

My husband Claude was 8th grade educated, son of a dirt farmer from rural Alabama, was a war hero. His family came from a long line of patriots. His father served in the Army in World War II, Korea, and Vietnam. I have seen all of my husband's military records, some original photos of his time in World War II, and his first Bronze Star, earned at 17 years old in the Battle of the Bulge. My oldest son, Larry, enlisted in the Marines and later served in Vietnam; my other son, Andy, enlisted in the Army, and when Larry returned, Andy spent 13 months in Vietnam. Five of my husband's ancestors served in the Civil War.

Claude was also an abusive alcoholic. My name is Dixie. My husband was a great provider, but when he drank alcohol, he could not keep his hands off me. I distinctly remember the abuse, as a direct result of the alcohol, from the time Larry was five years old, during our first tour in Germany, until he turned 20, when I *finally* divorced Claude. Despite many years of physical, mental, and verbal abuse, I remained in the marriage for my children: Larry, Andy, and my daughter Judy. I'm a little embarrassed to admit that we married seven days before Larry was born. We never told the children.

I was one of five children born to "land poor" parents in Eclectic, Alabama, about ten miles from Wetumpka. After high school in Eclectic, I worked part time as a telephone operator, living with my parents.

We were in Lawton, Oklahoma, when Claude went off to Vietnam in the spring of 1965. Peace at home finally: no fighting and no abuse. I remember all of the drinking, yelling, fighting, cursing, him beating me, and my children standing by crying and helpless.

When Claude returned from Vietnam in the spring of 1966, he wanted to pick up where he left off, drinking and abuse. I would not allow him in our home unless he promised to quit drinking. But Claude insisted on coming into our home and being allowed to drink — Larry was only 19 in the spring of 1966 and told his father that he would gladly step out into the front yard and fight him. Claude said, «Okay, smart ass, let's go."

I intervened and said, "Claude, that's enough!" I was afraid that my husband would have killed my son, but Larry felt since he had been the man of the house, he should stand up to his father. That was horrifying for me. I was shaken. Claude would not promise me that he would stop drinking, so he lived at Ft. Sill for some time.

In the spring of 1967, Claude asked for an "intervention,» and wanted the base chaplain at Ft. Sill to come to our home to "discuss this." I knew it was about the alcohol, drinking, and fighting, Claude's effort to put it straight, and to ask us face to face how we felt about this. I spoke with my children before the chaplain came to our home. I said, «It's your decision, but you know my position: your father won't stop drinking and he won't stop beating me."

When the chaplain arrived, Claude was in his best dress uniform. We did not sit down, as it did not take that long. Larry was almost 20, Judy was 18, and Andy was 16. The chaplain asked "if your father *promised* to stop drinking, could he come back into your home and your lives?" A lot of pressure was on the children, but the answer was unanimous. Larry told the chaplain, *and* looked into his father's eyes and said, "You can't stop drinking. You wanted to fight me over this a year ago. I do not want you here — in my life. You asked and that's how I feel." Judy and Andy concurred. Sad but true.

So many horror stories about the drinking and the abuse: I felt completely defenseless all those years. To help make ends meet, and ensure we could *eventually* own our own home in Lawton, I worked as a telephone operator and "nurse in training" during our assignments in El Paso (Ft. Bliss) 1955–1957, and then as a dental hygienist and office manager at Comanche County Memorial Hospital in Lawton, OK, 1960–1969. Upon arrival in Lawton in the summer of 1960, we lived in a very small home on 38th Street. I wanted a larger home since this would be at least a three-year assignment for Claude, and I did not know what was coming next. At 13 years old, Larry understood some of this, and he knew I did not want to go overseas again, ensuring the children could attend elementary school and into high school: junior high and high school — stability for the first time ever in our family life. I saved a lot of money, but Claude drank up a lot of it, too.

Larry followed in his father's footsteps and drank, but quit drinking on October 30th 1982, my birthday. He said he wished he had a nickel for every 20-cent beer he drank in Vietnam and on embassy duty in Ankara, Turkey. He did not seek out AA. He went cold turkey with the help of his wife. Larry never laid a hand on her. He has been sober and alcohol-free for 33 years.

Following our divorce, Larry, Judy, and I had no contact with Claude, until Larry went to Vietnam in late December 1969.

Claude knew Larry had enlisted in the Marines and Larry wrote him from time to time. Eleven months into his tour, his Battery 1st Sgt. came to Larry and said, "The Red Cross wants to know why you have not written your father. Your father got in touch with them and he thinks you have been killed." Larry told his 1st Sgt. that he had written his father several times but he never replied. His 1st Sgt. asked Larry to "please, write your father a letter today." When Larry came home from Vietnam, I told him that Claude had called, asking about Larry. I said, «You better call you damn father — he says he is concerned about you. I don't want to talk to him ever again about anything." Larry called him, let him know he was home and OK. Larry said that there was not much of a conversation from his side.

Martha

THE STORY OF
MARTHA

ADAM WAS EXCITING. He was known around town as a bad boy. I was known as a good girl. I fell head over heels. I was 18 and had moved out of my parents' house for the first time. Adam introduced me to drinking, dancing and parties. I got drunk for the first time. Eventually it was an every night thing. We lived in the fast lane.

I thought life was perfect until one night at a party, Adam's ex-girlfriend showed up. I watched out of the corner of my eye as they started kissing. I was really mad. I didn't make a scene. I just went out to our car and sat down. When I saw Adam come out, I could tell he was mad so I locked the door. He pounded on the door and kept screaming, "Open this door, bitch!" I was terrified, but finally unlocked the door. He pulled me out of the car by my hair and punched and kicked me.

Later, I got one of his friends to take me home. Physically I was hurt, but the biggest hurt was in my heart. I couldn't believe this had happened. The next day, Adam showed up and begged me to forgive him. He said he was sorry and promised it would never happen again.

I forgave him, hoping things could go back to the way they used to be. There was a couple of times he threatened me, but didn't hit me. When I found out I was pregnant, I thought we would be a big happy family. Adam seemed to be happy about becoming a daddy. That all ended when one night he got drunk and kicked me in the stomach because there was not enough money to buy even more beer. I miscarried.

The loss of my baby made me hate him. Adam said it was my fault. I was the one who made him mad enough to kick me. He kept telling me how much he loved me. I hoped he died. I called a local outreach ministry for help. They found a safe place for me to live and I moved out. I lived there until I could afford to move to another state. I never saw him again.

I would say to any woman who is being abused, swallow your pride and reach out to get help. There are people who will help you. I have since met a man who truly loves me. He treats me with kindness and respect. I love him and my life.

Sue Ellen

THE STORY OF
SUE ELLEN

My story is not remarkable, I do not think. I am sure it is more common than anyone cares to know. It does not make me remarkable and really, I am sure God had nothing to do with what happened to me except to get me through it. And for that I am so grateful.

My mom and dad were in love. They loved all of us kids. Then my daddy died. I was almost 5. He was 32. My mom had five kids, four of us were girls. Alice was 2, then me at 4, Stacy was 9, Lauren was 10 and my brother, Charles, was 15.

My mom went to work. My brother took care of us and we were OK.

Then about three years later my mother married my recently widowed uncle. Yes, she married her brother-in-law, Uncle Eric. And we thought it was great because we were little and Robert, Sharon and Stephanie were our favorite cousins.

Then my life changed. Eric was a police officer. They call them night watchmen in small towns. Everyone loved Eric. The mayor, the highway patrol, everyone. Still today, people tell me how Eric changed their life, set them on the right path. I have at least three male classmates that credit Eric for choosing law enforcement and they have had amazing careers.

Well, Eric molested all of my sisters and me. Not his daughters. Only his nieces.

My little sister and I didn't know it was happening to the older girls and vice-versa.

My older sisters left the house young, 15 and 16 years old. They got married to the first thing they could to get out. But Alice and I were young and we didn't understand that then.

No one talked about it.

I found out later that my older sister Stacy, who really acted out a lot in high school, went to tell the mayor. The mayor promptly called Eric and told him that Stacy was psychotic and saying crazy things. We needed to get her help. She got beat and locked in her room. I remember a dramatic episode where Stacy was really yelling at mom and I didn't understand why. I didn't correlate the connection of mother's blind eye to the abuse.

When I was 12, Alice was 10. We had moved to a new town. It stopped for a while. Then it started. Alice and I had begun going to church. We had a church family. Somehow that gave us the courage to talk to mom about it.

I remember the day like it was yesterday. We were sitting outside. Mom came up to us and said, and I hope everyone is sitting down for this, "He will leave if you want him to, but he will never bother you again."

I say, "Make him leave."

Alice says, "God forgives so we should forgive too."

Alice said what Mom wanted to hear, I guess. So he stayed. I wrote him a letter and told him if he touched my sister or me again, I would tell everyone about him. Everyone. He never touched me again. My sister however, tells me now that after I left home the following two years he abused her terribly. I wish I would have shot him.

The whole time, I never blamed my mom. I totally separated the issues. I had already lost my real dad and I refused to let Eric's sin take my mother from me. In the end, when he died at 70, I cried. I cried in relief, I cried in victory that I had my mother without him. I cried in mourning of my youth. I cried for what I wanted him to be and he just couldn't be. I just wanted a dad. It is what it is. I just didn't get one.

When he died, there were so many people at the funeral that they stood outside. He actually has an award for bravery. People today still come up when I visit back home and tell me what a great man he was. I just nod my head in silence to protect the innocent.

But, God did see me through and gave me insight to see through people. I have made so many mistakes. Is it because of the abuse I endured? Probably to a degree. I mean, how important are you when you are sacrificed for the comfort of the rest of the family? I didn't have a good example of who to choose nor did I know how to trust God to choose for me. God has loved me and carried me through all of my bad choices. He has been very merciful to me and He has blessed me with a good honest husband and father. I assure you I appreciate him as no one else can. I am so grateful to God for being my heavenly father and saving a wretch like me, truly.

My sister did not fare as well. She is an alcoholic now. She is 50, no children and a failed relationship of 13 years to a man she loved.

I still love my 81-year-old mother. I have told her I would not have handled it that way but I won't judge her. She is convinced the children would have been taken from her. Maybe he had her believing that, I don't know. And it's water under the bridge now. In the end, I have my mother, my sisters, my family, and my daughters, and my own father was a good man. I don't say anything about Eric because he has innocent daughters and they can't help that he was a monster.

Lynn

THE STORY OF
LYNN

I MET MY HUSBAND RYAN IN CHURCH. Everyone loved Ryan. He seemed to be the nicest guy in the world. When we announced our engagement, some of the church members shouted for joy. I was sure that I had met the man of my dreams.

One day we got into an argument over something petty. Ryan slapped me. I was in shock. My face hurt, but my feelings were hurt more. Ryan cried and said he was under a lot of stress. He said he would never raise a hand to me again.

Six months went by and he slapped me again. I told him I wanted a divorce. He said he would kill me before he would give me a divorce. Ryan made a good living as he had his own roofing company. I was a housewife who was dependent on her husband for food, clothes and a house. I no longer wanted to have sex with him, but he held me down and did it anyway.

I finally went to our pastor who called Ryan in to counsel us. Ryan denied everything and explained the bruise on my cheek was the result of a fall. I was in shock at this blatant lie and began crying hysterically. Ryan asked our pastor to pray for us. The pastor prayed and said that Satan was attacking our marriage. He had no idea that it was Satan through Ryan. Who Ryan was in public was completely different to who he was in private.

Because I no longer wanted to have sex with him, Ryan became insanely jealous. He was convinced that if I didn't want to have sex with him, I must be seeing someone else. He demanded to know where I was every minute of the day. The hitting continued. I noticed that he tried to hit me in such a way that it wouldn't leave a mark. We also continued with sex. Whenever he wanted it, he forced me.

Ryan started verbally abusing me, telling me how worthless I was and calling me names like ugly and fat. I began wondering if I was going insane as I started to fantasize about killing him. I thought about shooting him or stabbing him. I even considered poisoning him. When it came down to taking action, I knew I couldn't kill him. It just wasn't in me.

I became super depressed. Everyone at church including our pastor thought I was the problem in our marriage. I didn't have anyone to turn to who would believe my side of the story. I was miserable. My fantasies turned from killing him to killing me.

Both my parents were dead. The only other family I had was an older brother who I had never been close to. I couldn't think of anyone else I could turn to. When I called James, I was surprised at the warmth in his voice. Thank God, someone believed me!

The next day, James came and got me. We packed my stuff. Ryan showed up at the house while we were finishing up. He immediately went into his song and dance, but James told him to shut up. He told Ryan that he knew the truth and if Ryan ever bothered his sister again, he would kick his ass. Thanks to God and my brother, I now have peace in my life.

Angela

THE STORY OF
ANGELA

My mother was well known in our town and was highly thought of. When she was married to my birth father, she endured terrible things of abuse back in the 1930s and early 1940s. Back then, there was no such thing as a man being abusive. It was, "What did you do to make him hit you?" The things she told me, as an adult, were so sad. I did not get to be with her from age 6 till I turned 15. My birth father had threatened to kill all of us if she took me and my brother and left. You may not want the story, but it was through my life with my dad that I came to know the Lord, at age 11, much to his dismay, and had to resolve, as a young child, to live for *Jesus* the best I could. I can imagine what mother had to go through.

The 1930s and 1940s were still a time when men considered women only as teachers, nurses, or office help. Most men worked farms they owned, or had businesses in small communities. Since I was born in 1934, and my only sibling in 1932, I assume my mother was in her late teens when she married my dad, who was an only child, whose dad had deserted my grandmother. Maybe that is partly why he was such an angry, resentful man.

Daddy was a gun and camera enthusiast. He was a really strict disciplinarian who believed that no meant *no*, and his belt was punishment to me and my brother if we made him angry. Daddy left welts and you knew you better toe the line.

In a strange way, daddy loved me and my brother devotedly, but despised my mother. When we lived with daddy, he told us that if we ever saw our mother, we were to run screaming for help. My conversion, in a Pentecostal prayer meeting at age 11, inflamed him. He believed most all church folks were hypocrites. He named off the denominations and said they all believed they were right. If he leaned toward any that he had some confidence in, it was Full Gospel, or Pentecostals. He was raised Methodist.

His mother and her siblings owned land, stock, and did well in Central Texas. He would take us there to stay with them for weeks when he needed to be alone.

My mother's mother died when mother was 6 weeks old, and since her dad already had three children, he could not care for her. So he adopted her out to an elderly couple. When she married my daddy, she had no idea of the life she would have. Times were hard. Daddy broke my grandmother's will and sold her houses. The money was apparently squandered on radios, cameras, and guns.

He cursed really hard at all of us when he was mad. He had a hard time keeping a job, though I don't know why. He drank and that made it worse.

Mother threatened to take us and leave, but he said he would kill all of us if she did. I never saw my mother's bruises as I was so young, but then, he wanted her to prostitute herself to bring in money. When that happened, she left us and went away. She wanted to take us, but back then there was no such thing as "safe houses" or "shelters.» People back then, and even into the 1950s, would ask a woman "what she did to make her man mad enough to hit her." It was never his fault. Mother told me about the Christmases and birthdays that she sent us clothes and toys by way of one of daddy's aunts, but daddy never told us she sent them. I even described a dress, one Christmas, when I was 10, in Houston, and mother told me she sent it. I knew that mother could never reveal where she was, as daddy said he would kill her.

I remember so much about the life with my daddy, and most of the time, we had very little. I learned how to take care of myself and I learned skills that helped me earn a few dollars as I reached my early teens. When I was 14, I attended the Salvation Army Church in Amarillo. I worked in the school cafeteria for my lunches. Little did I know that my pastor of the church was working with my mother's sister in Houston to get me out of Amarillo and with my mother.

I checked out of school in early March, 1949, at age 15, and caught a Greyhound bus headed to Houston to meet my aunt. On the bus I had a comic book and the heroine was named "Angela." In Houston, my aunt and my mother met the bus. I was delirious with joy. She drove me to their house, where I met my stepfather, who welcomed me with all his heart. When I started school, mother asked me how I wanted to be known. I said, "Angela Smith," my stepdad's name, instead of Scott, my birth surname. My new school was the best school I ever attended and the most loving. I joined the Methodist Church across the street from where we had an apartment.

In the years that passed, after school and married, I reconnected with daddy but it was not always pleasant. When our daughter Kim was killed, daddy came to see us, as he had met her before, but his resentment had never softened. He even came to see a businessman here who was in the Lodge that my stepdad was in, and called my stepdad. My stepdad came to that business and they ordered daddy to leave if he did not want trouble. He did, but it was not pleasant.

In 1960 daddy passed away. I knew his resentment was very severe and wondered about his soul. In a dream, he came to me and showed me his scars of the autopsy, and said he was fine and well. I took that to believe that he finally made peace with our Lord. I just know my mother went through so much and was afraid of him.

Vivian

THE STORY OF
VIVIAN

So I have two stories about what abuse can do to a family. My mom and dad divorced when I was 8, and my mom later remarried. Clarence was nice at first, then he started drinking a lot. Later on he became very verbally abusive. They would fight a lot and he would verbally abuse her and leave for a few days. It continually got worse. She would ask me what she should do and I would *always* tell her to leave him. She never did, and I think in her mind she deserved it and thought she believed he was the best she could get.

After a while it became a pattern. My stepsister, who was 8 at the time, lived with them, and in 1985 it came to a sad end. While my sister was sitting in the front room she could hear them fighting, but this time it was more than just a fight. When Mom finally decided it was time to leave him, Clarence put a 22 pistol to her chest and shot her. I received a phone call that Mom was in the hospital so I rushed up to see her. When I got there it was too late. She was gone. A single gunshot to the chest. Her husband had taken her life.

That night he took everything she had to a pawn shop and hocked it all. The police were sure that it was a homicide but a judge ended up ruling it a suicide. The coroner said that because of the angle of the shot, there was no way it was self-inflicted. Still, overturned. The night of her viewing, Clarence went into the mortuary and took all of her jewelry off and stole it right out of the casket.

To this day, we have no idea where he is. It's been years since, and I finally asked my sister, who is now 38 years old, if she seen what had happened. She said without hesitating that he had shot her.

A few years after this my sister and her live-in boyfriend moved into the house right next to the one we grew up in. They eventually ruled them as common-law marriage because they lived with each other so long. I never seen them being violent with each other, but one Saturday I received a phone call from my sister, Lindsey, that my other sister, Donna, was found dead in their house. My dad was out of town and I had to be the one to contact him and let him know Donna was dead. She was found strangled to death in her front room. Her boyfriend said he had been in Salt Lake at the time of her death. The time was determined at around noon on a Saturday.

The neighbor said that was impossible because she was late for work and seen him coming from their back door at around 12:30. It went to trial and everyone knew he was guilty. The sad thing is it was determined she was also raped after she was killed. There was overwhelming evidence of his being guilty. I am not at all prejudiced but he was a black man and—at the time—they opted not to have a jury. The judge was removed from another county prior to this trial due to being prejudiced and it looks as though he didn't want that on him again. Every bit of evidence leaned to his being guilty. Even his work was there to terminate him based on a conviction but the judge ruled not guilty based on lack of evidence. When they read the ruling the guy stood up in court, flipped my dad off and walked out.

It took me months to convince my dad to not find the guy and kill him. It took its toll on my dad very much and he ended up passing away of a heart attack at age 55. It's been a tough road going through this. As each one of my sons grew to get married, I warned them that under *no* circumstances do they ever lay a hand on their wife or kids. I have seen it firsthand.

My daughter started dating a kid that I could see the same attributes in. I warned her and explained what happened to my mom and my sis. I could see the signs. It took a long time but she has finally removed him from her life.

I hope this in some way can help someone who is going through the same things. I can't stand by whenever I see a man being abusive to any lady or child. It's unacceptable at any level. I have shared my story many times. I feel that by doing so, and proving that you can make it through these trials, it makes me stronger and more sensitive to those who have gone through the same things.

Thank you for allowing me to share my story.

Helen

THE STORY OF
HELEN

My mother Helen married my father in 1947. My father was in the military, so we traveled all over the country as I was going up. They raised three children: my sister, brother and me. I think we were your normal family. I know I had a happy childhood.

My dad passed away in 2005. He had been in poor health for a number of years, worsening at the end. God says there is a season for all things, a time to live and a time to die. I wasn't saddened as much at my dad's passing as I was relieved. He knew Jesus so I felt he went to Heaven. My dad was a good man and father. My mother was a good woman and mother.

As with most widows, Helen had a hard time adjusting to life without her husband, who she had spent most of her adult life with. Loneliness is the hardest thing for most widows in her circumstances to deal with. Then, what seemed like a miracle happened. Since she was living in the town that she grew up in, she reconnected with an old schoolmate sweetheart, Gary.

Gary had never left their childhood community. He was a widower. Gary was retired from a successful business. He appeared to be able to provide for Helen financially and, more importantly, give her the companionship she needed. After meeting Gary, my siblings and I were supportive of their being together. After a short period of time, they married.

For the first couple of years, things couldn't have gone any better. We welcomed Gary into our family with open arms. Gary was friendly and always seemed to be glad to see us when we came to visit. My brother and his family who were from out-of-state were visiting Mother and Gary for the weekend. They had done this on several occasions, always with positive results.

The following Monday, I received a call from my brother. He asked me if I had ever heard Gary speak in a derogatory manner to our mother. I was a little shocked. I told my brother I had never heard Gary be anything but nice to Mother. My brother said Gary had spoken to Mother in a harsh and condescending way. On our next visit I was alert for any possible ugliness from Gary. There was none.

On my brother's next visit, it happened again and he told Gary not to speak to Mother like that. Gary exploded and told my brother to get out of his house or he would kill him. My brother, my sister and I were all shocked by his outburst. Mother finally confided in my sister that Gary talked that way to her all the time. Mother was ashamed, but coming from an earlier time in society, she felt like she just had to bear it.

We talked to her about leaving Gary, but she was reluctant to do so until Gary told her that my brother was no longer welcome in their home. That was one thing Mother could not bear, doing without her children. My sister went and picked her up on the pretense of visiting for the weekend which she had done in the past. Gary didn't know it, but Mother had already agreed that she was not going back.

When he found out that Mother wanted a divorce, Gary called and begged her to come back. He promised he would change. Mother could not forget that he had threatened to kill one of her kids.

IT'S NOT YOUR FAULT!

We arranged to come get her stuff as Gary agreed not to be there. I took a gun in case there were any more personality traits that we didn't know about. After they got divorced, Mother lived with my sister until her health required that she go into a nursing home.

This episode in our lives taught me that one never knows what is really going on behind a good front.

Paula

THE STORY OF
PAULA

So I'm not really sure how to start this since I have never written about this before. In fact, it's not something that I talk about very often. I come from a very large family and the majority of them are in the ministry. My grandpa was a deacon in his church and an interim pastor. My father was a pastor and my mother is an ordained minister. At one time, all but two of my dad's siblings were either pastors or married to one. So needless to say, I come from a family with strong Christian faith.

If my family and those who know my family knew my story, they would be shocked. My parents and siblings did not find out about this until I was 18 years old. Due to the size of my family, the majority of them do not know my story either, but I am not alone in the abuse that I endured.

I spent most if not all of my free time at my grandparents' house. All of my memories regarding my grandma are of her being sick. I loved my grandma and I would go to her house every day after school and most of the weekend to help her clean her house, wash clothes, make sure she had taken her medication, etc. I did whatever I thought was going to help her live because I did not want her to die. She had multiple heart attacks during this period of time which was one of the reasons I was always at her house. I probably spent more time at their house than any other family member during this time.

As an adult, I have come to the conclusion that she must have known what was going on and she did nothing to my knowledge to stop it from happening. I can't say that I blame her or have any harsh feelings towards her, but in the same breath I cannot fathom why she would allow this to happen to me for such a long period of time. But then again, her health was not good and as an adult I tend to think she did not have the strength or the drive to fight.

The abuse in my life began when I was 9 years old and continued until I was 13 years old. It wasn't until I was 15 or so that I realized that I had been molested or sexually abused. You did not hear about this sort of stuff—it wasn't talked about amongst family, friends, on the TV or news like it is today.

I was sexually abused by my paternal grandfather. I can remember the day it began as if it were yesterday. We had had a family gathering at my grandparents' house. After most everyone had left, I was sitting on the couch in my grandfather's lap when he stuck his hand down the back of my pants and was feeling my butt cheeks. My bottom was cold and he whispered in my ear "I know how I can warm you up." I honestly don't know what my reaction was when he said this.

My grandpa took me out to his shop which was a café at one time. In the back end of the café was the kitchen area with a little cubby area sort of like a closet. In that cubby he had an old mattress laid on the floor that I had not seen in there before. Now, this part of his shop was not clean. It was cluttered, dusty, and had cobwebs everywhere. He told me to lie down on the mattress and he would warm me up but it was "our secret" and went on to tell me "if you ever tell anyone our secret, I will tell them that you are the one who asked for this." Naturally, only being 9 years old,

I had no idea what he really meant when he said this but I will never forget what happened next. This was the day my innocence was stolen from me.

Let's just say that I learned more than some adults know about foreplay, intercourse, oral and anal sex at 9 years old. I also learned about feeling guilty, responsible, dirty, and ugly. On top of those feelings, I learned to lie and to be convincing. During the three, almost four years of abuse, I also learned to be a protector for my sister and other female cousins. Even though I really didn't know that what he was doing wasn't acceptable, I knew that I didn't want any of them to experience the things he had done to me. When I thought that he might be "interested" in one of them, I would make myself available to him by what I learned later is "coming on or flirting" with him to draw his attention to me.

Due to this abuse, he also taught me to masturbate, long before I ever heard or knew what that word meant. And every time that I would get the desire to do so, I felt really dirty. I had no idea why I felt the urge to do it but I did. I had to sneak around so that my parents and siblings would not catch me doing this because of the things my grandpa would say to me about it being my fault.

As you can imagine, this has caused a multitude of issue in my life. I have issues putting my trust in men and people in general. I have issue with giving anyone control over my life, emotions, body, money—really any control. I am not an emotional person. I do not experience the feelings of excitement, extreme joy, sadness, and grief. I rarely cry. In fact, I hate to cry. If you make me cry, you have done something bad to me or my family or you have really pissed me off. I think this is because I did not dare show any emotions when I was a child for fear of someone finding out what I had done and the punishment I would get for doing it. To this day, I do not have deep emotional ties with many in my life.

I believe that due to having parents who prayed consistently, those prayers have protected me from ever experimenting with illegal drugs. I am not an alcoholic. I do not care for the taste of alcohol and I do not like feeling out of control that comes with too much consumption. I will have a mixed drink from time to time. Unlike most victims of sexual abuse, I have had very few sexual partners.

There was always tension between my parents and grandparents for as long as I can remember. I'm not really sure why, but they did not get along very well. For many years I thought that this was the reason that my grandpa "chose" me. I felt he did it as a way to hurt my parents, but I found out later that he did things to some of my cousins as well. However, it was not to the extent of what he did to me. I also suspect that he sexually abused at least one of his daughters, but that is purely an assumption. So it was about his sick need to control someone.

I have been married a few times to men I had no business being with. I married my first husband at 18 years old and we were married almost 13 years. We were young and I wanted out of my parents' house. After we had children I learned that he had sexual and porn addictions and would force sex on me which I later learned was considered rape (even though we were married). The next one was a master manipulator, control freak, verbally and mentally abusive and was physically abusive *one time*. After twenty months of marriage, this is when I knew I could not stay married to him. My current husband also has many addictive behaviors (alcohol and tobacco) and issues with control. This has caused problems and stress in our marriage. My mother-in-law was the meanest, most hateful, loveless, and controlling woman I have ever met. He is a product of his environment as am I.

IT'S NOT YOUR FAULT!

I struggle with feeling like a failure. I struggle with being completely honest and have to make a conscious effort not to tell a lie. I hate feeling out of control or feeling as if someone is trying to control me. I think I am a fixer. I think that I can fix anything in any situation and any person. I am not a people pleaser and I do not care what you think about me.

Ashley

THE STORY OF
ASHLEY

I ONLY GO INTO DETAIL about the courtship because I think it's relevant to understanding how the pattern of abusive personality is already present, but abusers can be very charming and hide their ugly sides well—at first.

I met Gary at a party. We flirted a bit, but I was very unsure of him. I knew everyone in the area, but he was a newcomer. He had moved from a big city to our small town for work. He was 19, I was 16. Gary began pursuing me relentlessly, tracking me down, getting my phone number from friends. He began showing up wherever I was. He was very charming and won me over. We began to date a few weeks later.

I was very naïve about relationships, having only gone as far as kissing with some of the local boys. Gary was very patient with me, waiting until I was ready to carry the relationship further.

I later learned that he most definitely wasn't waiting around. He was sleeping with a multitude of women. I didn't recognize this as the first warning sign of trouble, even after I was slapped in the face with the reality. Gary later told me that he was initially drawn to me because, even though I ran with the party crowd, I was still "pure." To him, I later discovered, I was something to be obtained, that would always be his and only his to control.

Little did I know that after he would escort me home after a date he would drive to the nearby apartment of a friend where he would stay up all night doing drugs, drinking heavily, and participating in "sex-ed," a game that consisted of two girls who would expose themselves to the men and "educate" them on female anatomy. I only include this because I think it reflects the dual personality Gary had, a true Jekyll-and-Hyde. The sweet gentleman by day and the deeply disturbed addict by night.

During this time I began to notice that Gary was rarely without a drink in his hand, but I came from parents who didn't drink so I had no understanding of alcoholism. His drink of choice was vodka and grapefruit juice. To this day the smell of it makes me physically ill. But I chalked it up to youthful partying and thought he would outgrow it.

If I hadn't been so naïve I might have noticed the first major signs of trouble at this time. Gary became less attentive, focusing his attention on other females in our group. He seemed enthralled when they flirted with him, and I began to doubt myself compared to these experienced girls. Abusers have a way of spotting vulnerable souls, people with insecurities, and using that to their advantage in order to exert control.

I began to get reports from my friends that Gary was having sex with at least three girls from my school. At first I didn't want to believe, but eventually I wised up and broke up with him. I should have recognized the behavior that followed as stalking and obsessive but I mistook it for true love.

Immediately after the breakup, Gary began to call my personal phone hourly during the day as well as during the middle of the night, presumably to make sure I was home. This was before caller ID or cell phones. Gary began to drive by my house repeatedly, send me flowers, and leave cards and notes on my car. He would follow me on dates with other boys, so that they became uncomfortable. I finally gave in and decided he must truly love me, so we resumed the relationship.

For several months he was wonderfully attentive, doting on me constantly. Little did I know, it only took him a couple of weeks to return to his late night party habits, but somehow he managed to be discreet enough to keep me from learning of it.

After about ten months, near the end of my senior year after I'd turned 17, he proposed by giving me a lovely diamond and pledging his undying love to me. I accepted the proposal, even though my parents were very disapproving, and we were married four months later. We took a short honeymoon, where the first signs of abuse began. During the honeymoon he drank heavily and would become belligerent if any man spoke to me. Once he even got into a shoving match with a man who offered to give me his seat so I wouldn't have to stand. I realized quickly that the best way to avoid such confrontation was to just avoid talking to other men, or doing anything that would attract their attention.

Shortly after our marriage, Gary began to beg me to get pregnant. Another warning sign I didn't see coming: getting me pregnant would ensure that I was tied to him. Within four months of our wedding I was pregnant. My father bought us a home and gave Gary a fantastic job. Gary resented that for the remainder of our marriage, and he carried a huge chip on his shoulder all the time because people at work would tease him about being the boss man's son-in-law. The men at his job had known me for years—I was like their own daughter—and Gary was extremely jealous of that. When they would speak to me or ask about me he would come home and explode, accusing me of having had some sort of sexual relationship with them in the past, even though he knew that wasn't the case. Abusers are *very* insecure.

Eventually some of the people I knew told me that he was sleeping with two women at work while I was at home very sick with my pregnancy. My parents no longer paid my car payment and Gary convinced me to sell the car to save money for the baby. To please him, I did. It solved the problem of him accusing me of slipping off to sleep with other men during the day while he was working hard, in my sick pregnant state.

Soon a pattern developed of Gary spending most of his paycheck on alcohol (my parents paid our mortgage and bills most of the time), not coming home until 2-3 a.m. and eventually not coming home at all, leaving me at home with no groceries. I was not allowed a phone because he felt I would just call men or my girlfriends, which he thought were all whores. I lost contact with everyone and became very isolated. I learned he warned people not to come to the house if he wasn't home, and he had a reputation for being a very mean drunk so no one wanted to go against him.

When Gary did come home he was typically drunk on a nightly basis, and would pick fights. He had a very volatile temper and would throw/break things. I had to keep the house spotless or he would become completely unglued. Once he came home after I had spent all day cleaning and found I had not put the vacuum cleaner back in the closet yet, so he promptly picked it up and threw it through a glass door.

Gary began to invite people over to party at our home every weekend. Sometimes they would stay for 24-48 hours gambling, drinking and who knows what else. I could barely rest because of the noise. I learned to keep my eyes downcast when I was around others, because even just making brief eye contact with a man could cause me to undergo hours of being subjected to shouting and screaming.

Gary's favorite game was mind battering. I wasn't allowed to sleep when these episodes would start, and he literally could spend four, five, even six hours pinning me against a wall while he cursed, belittled, ranted… Sometimes he wouldn't allow me to go to the bathroom, once resulting in me urinating on myself. I was too embarrassed to tell anyone what was happening. I honestly had no idea what was happening. I'd never even heard of spousal abuse. All I knew is that this wasn't how my parents behaved.

Early into this abuse cycle I threatened to leave, and was met with the first of threats against my family. "If you leave, I'll just got out there and beat the shit out of your dad." How do you react to that, when you've seen this person beat the shit out of guys just for looking at you? I couldn't take the chance he would hurt my father, so I said nothing.

I gave birth to our son, four weeks premature. The baby and I both stayed in the hospital for a week. Gary would visit for a short time each evening and then leave to who knows where. It was the most peace I'd had in a long time so I enjoyed it. On the day we were discharged, Gary did not show up to get us. *My* mother came and took us to her home. Gary didn't show up for three days. I later learned he had two girls staying at our house while I was in the hospital and was on a long drug and alcohol binge. I knew about the alcohol but I didn't know that he had begun to shoot methamphetamine. I never saw the needle marks.

After being called a whore, an idiot, the most stupid person on earth, being told "no one else will ever want you, you're worthless" over and over and over, it began to become the reality for me. I no longer wore makeup or did my hair because it attracted looks from men. I no longer made eye contact. I didn't tell anyone what was happening. Why risk him hurting my family? I began to fear interacting with all men, as though I was doing something wrong and wasn't a good wife.

As anyone knows who suffers abuse, the abuser usually begins his cycle of attack with mental manipulations, creating an enormous sense of worthlessness, helplessness and fear in order to maintain control.

Gary began to believe that working for my father and living in a town where my family was prominent in the community was the cause for all his unhappiness. So we moved to the city near his family. I will not speak about Gary's childhood, why he developed the cycle of alcoholism and abuse, because I have a close relationship with his family now and do not want to hurt them.

Once we moved, the abuse escalated rapidly. In my hometown, the police knew my family well and now I realize Gary was afraid of that. In the city, my family had no authority. Upon moving to our new home there were new rules. I was allowed no car and no phone, as before. But now I was also not allowed shoes. This was so I could not run away. Food was controlled based on my "behavior." If I did everything right and didn't make him angry, he would allow me to buy food. If I made him angry, which breathing could do when he was drinking, I was told I was too fat and didn't deserve food (at that timed I'd lost from 100 pounds when we started dating to 90 pounds).

One evening Gary's sister came by and wanted me to go with her to the store. When we returned ,Gary thought we'd been gone too long and accused us of meeting men. He picked me up and tried to toss me off the second floor balcony. Thankfully, his sister fought him tooth and nail, saving my life.

One night Gary came home from work early and I had walked to the park next door with our son so he could play. When I got back to the house Gary was waiting at the door. He called me a whore and punched me in the face. The next thing I knew I was on my back and he was straddling me, choking me. I remember I couldn't breathe. I could see spots in front of my eyes and my nose was bleeding heavily. Somehow I was able to kick him in the groin and crawled out the door. Our son was screaming and he grabbed him before I could take him. I bolted down the sidewalk and ran to the neighbors. I called the police and my parents. My parents arrived before the cops (they lived an hour away and beat the cops—go figure).

My mother wouldn't let my dad get out of the car because Gary was screaming that he would kill my father. My mother calmly walked up to the door and demanded that Gary give her our son. He stepped out and raised a hand to her. I watched in horror, waiting for him to strike, but she struck first. She began to beat him about the head with her purse. He was wailing and cowering. The cops pulled up then, and she began screaming that he was assaulting her. A wonderful moment in all this was watching my mother beat the crap out of this guy! I think he didn't hit her in return because my father had stepped out of the car with his pistol, and no matter what Gary said later, I learned he was scared to death of my dad.

As the police took Gary away my mom opened her purse and revealed that she had emptied it and then filled it with ball bearings! Good for her! My nose was broken, and I had strangle marks around my throat. My parents had to stop the car twice on the way to their home so I could vomit from nerves. Luckily our son was unharmed.

For three months I began to rebuild my life. My father bought me a car, rented me a home, and helped me get a job. My son was doing well in daycare. And suddenly Gary reappeared. He begged me and my parents for another chance to be a father to our son and asked for our help to stop drinking. Through it all I did love the man, and that's hard for people to understand. See, when a drunk is drinking they can be mean as hell, but when they are sober they are charming, disarming, and very, very *sorry*. There is no one more repentant than a drunk that's sober.

Here is also where people ask, *why?* Why would you let this man back into your home? Because! Because I truly believed everything he had drummed into my head for two years: I was worthless, no one else would ever want me, I was stupid, I was ugly. Shall I go on?

As soon as Gary moved back in, the cycle began again. Right away he let me know that he would not only kill my father, but also my mother *and our son* if I ever tried to leave him again. Sadly, I knew at this point he wasn't bluffing about our son. He swore to me that if we couldn't be a family together he would *kill* our son because he knew it would hurt me more than anything else on earth.

One day I was late getting off work. My car had a T-top. Gary came to my job, and when I walked out to get into my car he was waiting. He walked over and began shouting. I had the windows rolled up and doors locked but the T-top was off so he reached in and grabbed the back of my hair, pulling it out by the roots. My scalp bled. My hair didn't grow back in that spot for several years.

He began showing up drunk at my office almost every day. Finally, my boss let me go. He said they just couldn't have that going on at a business, and I don't blame him one bit. Gary was so happy. I have no doubt he did it on purpose. Almost daily I endured slaps, shoves, punches, kicks, and so on. Gary would hold knives to my throat and threaten to slit it. This always occurred after he was drinking, of course.

I had had a phone installed at the house, and girls who had been friends of mine in school would call to see what I was doing. Gary became very angry about these calls. I thought that it was weird also, but it took me a little while to figure out they were calling to see if he'd left home yet, that he was supposed to be meeting them.

Finally, one night when this happened I decided to follow him to see what was really going on. I found him parked, getting into the car of the girl that had called. I pulled up and caught him red-handed. It was the first time I was brave enough to confront him.

Our son was in the carseat beside me. I drove back home with Gary following me. I unloaded our son from the car and took him into the house. Gary came barreling in behind me. I grabbed our son and ran to the other side of the living room. Gary picked up our large coffee table and hurled it at me. Trying to protect our son, I stuck my leg out to stop the table. The result was a bone sticking out of the top of my foot. Of course I'm crying, our son is crying. Gary takes our son, tosses him on the couch, and grabs a pillow to put over my face so I would stop crying. So I was pinned on the floor, pillow pressed to my face and cannot breathe. I'm having to fight him with an already broken foot that is bleeding everywhere.

Finally our son toddled over and grabbed his dad by the hair. Gary released me and I finally could breathe but didn't dare make a sound, so I choked back my tears. He realized there was no way out of this, I had to go to the hospital. He asked a neighbor to watch our son and put me in the car.

The ER doctor recognized what was going on right away. I had bruises all over my body in different stages of healing, obvious signs of abuse. I had a busted lip and red rash all over my face from the pillow. Not to mention the bone sticking out of the top of my foot and the swelling and bruising to that entire leg. Gary refused to leave me alone with the doctor. I was mentally begging the doctor to kick him out, to call the cops, but I couldn't say anything because I would have gotten it ten times worse later if I had, which means I most likely would have wound up dead.

The ER doctor got very close to me and asked me, "Is there anything you want to tell me?" He knew, I could see it in his eyes, but I didn't dare say anything. At that moment I really thought, this is it. I'm going to die like this and no one is ever going to help me.

Luckily the bone that had popped out had popped back in so I didn't require surgery. The ER doctor sutured the wound closed and put a cast on me. I was sent home on crutches with some pain pills.

When we arrived home Gary wouldn't help with our son, so I had to hobble around that night and bathe him, feed him and get him to bed. I wondered what that girl would think if she knew that the act of me catching my husband in her car had resulted in this. Would she still want to be with him knowing this? Would she care about me?

I knew if I told my parents what happened they would intervene, and now I truly believed that Gary would follow through on his threats to murder them and our son if I ever told, so I remained silent. Gary took away my pain pills, saying I was a junkie if I took them. But he took them. He said it was my own fault I had a broken foot. For the next few weeks, every time he became angry he would kick my cast.

The breaking point came one night when a very sweet girl from my graduating class invited me to a party at her parent's new home. Everyone I'd known for years would be there, all my old friends, and I just wanted to feel normal for one night. So Gary agreed, and we went to the party. Gary brought along one of his drinking buddies. Of course they drank heavily, and at one point during the night I found myself sitting in the living room talking to a boy from school that had been a dear friend. Out of the corner of my eye I saw Gary approach with a golf club. Before I could do anything he began to beat that boy. I ran to another room and called the sheriff's department. I had my husband and his friend arrested for assault. I had to beg the deputies not to tell him that I was the one who had called the police—I knew I would die for it. The poor boy had to have surgery on his face, the beating was so bad. And all because he innocently spoke to me. I've never forgotten that or forgiven myself for putting him in that situation.

I decided I wasn't going to bail Gary out of jail. I wouldn't answer the phone because I knew it was him calling. The entire next morning the phone continued to ring but I ignored it. I finally answered and was surprised to hear my father's voice. He had bailed Gary out and they were at my parents' home. I was *terrified*. But dad said Gary was so sorry—of course he didn't tell dad he nearly killed a boy—and wanted another chance.

The deal that was made was that he would attend AA regularly. Gary agreed and began to go to their meetings. Of course, he wanted me there and was thoroughly mad to learn that I couldn't be in the room with him, but rather I would be in the Al-Anon meeting for significant others.

I credit Al-Anon with saving my life. You see, they don't sit around and moan about how abused they are. Instead, they teach you that your life is important, that you are NOT responsible for the alcoholic or their actions, that you have a life to lead and you need to do so no matter what the alcoholic does. The alcoholic can either come along for the ride or stay behind. I began to grow courage, something I'd been lacking, and see the light at the end of the tunnel.

Finally, I was brave enough to escape. I took our son, went to my parents and told them everything. They were wonderful. My father hired off duty deputies to guard our home and escort me to and from school (I enrolled in college) and anywhere else I wanted to go. I was so fortunate to have a family that could provide this protection for me, but unfortunately the protectors couldn't be with me 24/7.

I filed for divorce. Gary began dating an old high school girlfriend, and they married after just a couple of months. We shared visitation with our son. Things continued to be rocky, as Gary would call any man I dated at home and scream. He would also call me during the night if our son cried, demanding I take care of him. He would also tell me that he was just waiting, some day he would get his chance when I wasn't surrounded by cops.

Gary's new wife rented them a home in the city, but they split after only a couple of months due to abuse. I wasn't aware that she, the only stable thing in his home, had left. Gary called me to say they had a present for our son's birthday and would I pick it up from their home? I was in the area, and alone. But I agreed because I knew his wife would be home at that time, she always was.

When I arrived around 4 p.m. I rang the doorbell. Gary opened it holding a loaded shotgun, pointed at my chest. What transpired next is a day/night I will never forget. Gary made me walk into the living room, where he made me stand in the corner while he sat on the couch, chugging a drink and pointing the loaded gun at me. He ranted, he raved, and he told me of his plan. He was going to kill me. But first he was going to drive me to my parents' home, kill them in front of me, then kill me in front of our son (he was with my parents).

He stood up and walked toward me, putting the barrel of the gun to my forehead. I remember thinking, this is it. It's finally going to happen. But he just laughed and walked back to the couch. Then he reached under the couch and pulled out a revolver.

He opened it and showed me that there were two bullets in the six-shooter.

Thus began the game of Russian roulette. Three times I was forced to kneel on the floor while he spun the chamber, put the gun to my temple and pulled the trigger. *Three times* I had to hear the click. There are no words to describe this.

And as I write this, I realize this is the very first time I have ever told the entire story to anyone other than my mother, my attorney, and the police. I've told bits and pieces to family and friends, but most people have the attitude of "why are you telling me this? I don't want to hear this." Even now, no one wants to hear about it. But if they thinks it's painful to hear about, they should think about what it was like to live it.

After the game of Russian roulette he allowed me to go to the bathroom. I was sick to my stomach and had to vomit. He made me take a shower then while he sat on the toilet with the pistol. After he wouldn't allow me to dress. He made me walk to the bedroom where he forced me to have sex with him.

I have to pause here because I am crying and shaking as I force myself to relive this nightmare…

After, he wouldn't let me have my clothes. He made me kneel on the bedroom floor in front of him while he stuck a needle in his arm. I guess he figured it was safe to put down the gun because I was naked and was too far from any exit anyway to outrun him. He told me it was meth and heroin in the syringe, that this is what I'd driven him to. Little did I know that this shot was what would save me.

He told me to get dressed so we could go to my parents. I noticed he was nodding off as I dressed so I calculated that in a few more minutes he might be too slow and uncoordinated to catch me if I ran for it. He took the pistol and made me walk back to the living room. At this point he could barely walk, so he plopped down on the sofa. What he didn't realize is that now I was closer to the door… but also very close to the shotgun.

Here was the big defining moment. I knew guns—I'd been raised around them my whole life—and for a minute, maybe two, I thought *pick up the shotgun and shoot him now, before he has the chance to kill your family.* And I almost did it, almost… but I thought of our son.

No father, dead, and a mother in prison. Plus then I would be like Gary. That thought turned my stomach. So instead I turned and ran. I jumped straight over the porch railing and sprinted down the block. I could hear Gary behind me. He stopped in the yard and began shooting the pistol but I was already gone, disappeared behind a row of bushes three houses down. I saw a car coming up the street and managed to flag them down. Gary had already gone back into his house. The cops weren't able to find him after.

Knowing I was in danger, and at the recommendation of my parents' attorney, they hid me in an apartment in the city while my son remained with my parents. The attorney and police felt that if Gary found me he would most definitely kill me, and my son if he was with me. The attorney got an emergency hearing with the court to remove all parental rights from Gary.

In the meantime, Gary was staying with the ex-wife of an old friend of his, who was also having custody issues. Gary called me out of the blue, no idea how he got my unlisted number, and told me that the ex-husband of the woman he was staying with was coming to get her child and he was going to kill him just like he was going to kill me. I was able to get ahold of the old friend and warn him *not* to go over there, that it was an ambush, and he was able to tell me where Gary was so the authorities could serve papers. Gary was served later that night and was to appear in front of the judge the next day.

Late that night someone went to my parents' home and blasted out all the windows with a shotgun, nearly killing my son. The next day in court Gary was sent to jail. It was to be the last time I saw him for many years. Gary was never allowed to have my address or phone number. His parents were awarded visitation but he never regained any parental rights.

He only served three months in jail but apparently was a model prisoner. My father paid him a visit in jail, his only visitor, and I'm told by the deputies that the conversation went like this: "You ever touch my daughter or anyone in my family again and I'll kill you myself." Apparently Gary took my father as the man of his word that he was. He left me and my family alone.

Of course I was not able to include all the incidents of abuse in this, but tried to highlight certain instances. To this day I still have nightmares. Typically they're about the sense of being trapped, no way out. I have had dreams where I am strangled to death. The nightmares once occurred nightly, now it's about once a year. I am now very strong-willed, almost harsh at times, but that happens after abuse. You either get busy living or get busy dying. You either break the cycle or repeat it again.

No one tells me what to do, what to wear, who to talk to. I have my own bank account, I have a successful career. I am not stupid, I am not worthless, I am not ugly. I am a survivor.

THE AUTHOR WEIGHS IN

While I was aware of abuse towards women, I didn't realize the number of women involved was so prevalent. It seems that almost everyone has been touched by it—if not themselves, then through a family member or friend.

The single biggest question that I previously had on the subject (I suspect a lot of others have the same) is: If you're being abused (physically, sexually or mentally), why don't you just get out? When some women in that situation are asked that, they don't give a response that makes much sense to an outsider. Even when she is in fear of her life, you would think she could find a way to leave.

It's just not that simple. There are a myriad of reasons that make sense to her, but may not to others. Unless you have been in her shoes, it is difficult to understand the emotions that she is going through.

I think it all starts with the way women are valued by not only our society, but the world in general. From birth a woman's worth is tied up in her looks. A man's looks are a minor factor. With a woman, her attractiveness is number one, every other aspect comes behind that. This is drummed into her every day by TV shows, movies and even her own peer group.

If she feels like she doesn't measure up physically (and I think most women feel that way) and as incredible as it might sound, a woman in an abusive relationship may subconsciously think she deserves the abusive treatment.

We can and need to do all we can to help abused women, but I'm not sure any real changes can be made until we change our value system. It starts with when our daughters are born. Somehow we must teach them that looks are secondary. Other elements of who they are are more important, such as their character. This is not an easy thing to do. You're up against an entire world. You might take a break, but the world never stops.

HOW DO I GET HELP?

If you are in immediate danger, please: **Call 911**.

Federal assistance

Call the U.S. National Domestic Violence Hotline:
1-800-799-7233 (SAFE), or
TTY 1-800-787-3224.

Call the U.S. National Sexual Assault Hotline:
1-800-656-4673 (HOPE)
The NSAH automatically connects you to a local U.S. rape crisis program based on the area code of your phone number.
http://www.nrcdv.org/dvam/safety-alert

Secure, online private chat is available at:
https://ohl.rainn.org/online

State assistance

I am listing my state. To find your state, Google "help for abused women in (your state)"

Texas Council on Family Violence
512-794-1133
http://www.tcfv.org

County assistance

I am listing my county. To find your county, Google "help for abused women in (your county)"

Wise Hope Shelter & Crisis Center
940-626-4855
http://www.wisehope.org

Additional helpful websites

Leaving Abuse
http://leavingabuse.com

Domestic Abuse Intervention Services
http://abuseintervention.org

ACKNOWLEDGEMENTS

I am grateful for the constant support of my wife, Tina, and my children: Jacob, Caleb, and Sarah.

Thank you to Missy Brewer for editing this book, to Michael Campbell for the book design, and to Bryan Gehrke for the cover design.

You can email me at williamjoinerauthor@gmail.com.

Learn more at
www.williamjoinerauthor.com

Joining the Rewards Club on my website is 100% FREE and scores you a FREE eBook copy of *American Entrepreneur.* As a Rewards Club member you will receive monthly notices of future give-a-ways and special promotions. My pledge to you is you won't receive an email from me more than once a month.

OTHER BOOKS BY
WILLIAM JOINER

American Entrepreneur
An Autobiography

Don't Let the Man Keep You Down
How to Start and Operate Your Own Business

Life Begins at Sunrise
An Inspiring Story of Love, God, Bird Dogs,
Walking Horses and Field Trials

The Legend of Jake Jackson
The Last of the Great Gunfighters and Comanche Warriors

The Blood Warrior
Revenge of the Timber Wolf

Mountain Girl
Called Home

Rowdy Remington
The Forgotten Cowboy

Running with Horses
A Story of Love and Murder

Recollections
Gunsmoke, Wildcats and the Day I Whooped the TV Preacher

www.williamjoinerauthor.com

Printed in Great Britain
by Amazon